An Anthology of Kids Poetry...

आज़ाद परिन्दे

...Born to fly

Vol. II

An Anthology of Kids Poetry...

आज़ाद परिन्दे

...*Born to fly*

Vol. II

Author
All Contributors

Highbrow Scribes Publications
New Delhi

An Anthology of Kids Poetry...
आज़ाद परिन्दे ...*Born to fly* Vol. II

*Published 2023 by Highbrow Scribes Publications
Printed in New Delhi, India*

ISBN: 978-81-956557-4-8

*Highbrow Scribes Publications's mission is to foster a universal
passion for reading by partnering with authors to help create stories
and communicate ideas that inform, entertain, and inspire, and to
connect them with readers everywhere.*

Highbrow Scribes Publications books are printed on acid-free paper.

www.highbrowscribes.com

Contents

बधाई एवं शुभकामनाएँ

‘वो परियों की जादुई कहानी,

जो तुम्हारे दिल को छू जाती थी,

सर्द मौसम मे ठंडा पानी,

जिसे पीकर छींक तुम्हे आती थी

कितनी मासूम है ख्वाहिश तुम्हारी,

शब्दो मे गढ़कर सुकुन जो पाती थी।

बहुत गर्व की बात है कि क्षितिज...व्येर ड्रीम मीट रियलिटी के अंतर्गत हम देश के कोने-कोने से आए चुनिंदा नन्हे कलमकारों का ये सांझा संकलन ला रहे हैं।

इतनी खूबसूरत रचनाओं द्वारा नवोदित कवि-कवयित्रियों को अपनी काव्य कौशल को उजागर करने का जो अवसर मिला है,उससे ना सिर्फ इन बच्चों मे आत्मविश्वास आएगा बल्कि अपनी कला सृजन को नये आयाम देने की दिशा मिलेगी।

इस पुस्तक को संकलित करने का मेरा अनुभव बेहद भावनात्मक रहा है।मुझे पुरी उम्मीद है की ‘आज़ाद परिन्दे -बोर्ड टू फ्लाय’ भाग 2 इन नए रचनाकारों के लिए मील का पत्थर साबित होगी।सम्पूर्ण क्षितिज परिवार की ओर सचिन मेधावी बच्चों को उनके उज्जवल भविष्य की ढेर सारी शुभकामनाएं।

श्रीमती रंजीता सहाय अशेष

संस्थापिका - क्षितिज...व्येर ड्रीम मीट रियलिटी

Publisher's Note

Life is all about the various stages and their ups and downs. Of all the stages, childhood is a time when we live freely at our behest. It is a time when a child explores his/her inner and outer self but with a free mind.

When we were approached to publish the free minds of these children, we were awe-struck at their voices. Each child has shown concern through his/her words and rhythmic styles about the various aspects of life, be it nature, patriotism, animals, relations and many alike. Especially when I read the poetries by two six-year-old girls, I was amazed as that age is meant for fun and frolic and not to play with words.

Our world revolves around our children. They make the foundations of our society and if the foundation is strong, we are bound to excel. Exploring the minds of these children gives us a way to even explore ourselves. They are a guiding light to us in their own ways. And that's how 'Azaad Parinde' makes its way for everyone to be the one and give life its best.

We wish each child the very best in their respective lives. May they keep on enlightening humanity through their wisdom and wise words and create a lasting impact on society as a whole.

Happy reading!

Vandana Bhatia Palli
Founder-Publisher
Highbrow Scribes Publications

Foreword

As an avid reader, I got the opportunity to read the poems of "Aazaad Parinde". I have been totally amazed by the works of these budding poets. I was approached by Ranjeeta Ma'am to write a preface for this book - at first, I thought how could I do justice to such an enthralling collection of poems. Each has its own voice, tone setting and message.

The bond of friendship in Kajal Singh's poem "Yaad ho tum sab" is so apt and thought-evoking ". Metamorphosis: True Beauty of Aradya Pandey is so crisp, appealing and full of beautiful imagery. The amazing use of poetic devices by Medanssh in "Life is all about certificates" is mesmerizing. The depth at that raw age of six, Shubra Shukla's "Ghar" epitomizes the empathy children have.

"Aao-bachaye apni dharti" from Bhavya emphasizes the fact that "we have not inherited this earth from our forefathers but borrowed it from our children". These contemporary budding stars have evoked deep thoughts indeed.

My heartiest congratulations to all of them for this unique effort. Each read is so subtle, picturesque and delightful. I wish them all happiness and prosperity in all they do.

Dr. (Smt) Rina Pathak

Principal, Seth M.R. Jaipuria School, Goel Campus, Lucknow
Registered Poet, Asst. Secretary Zone-3, CBSE Sahodaya,
Prayog CBSE Resource Person

Review

'Azaad Parindey' is a poetic compendium by 'Kshitij - Where Dreams Meet Reality' founded by Ranjeeta Sahay Ashesh. This anthology contains 21 poems by 21 children from India and abroad and is a reflection of the upcoming generation's mind. To put it mildly, it is a source of positive vibes when there is so much strife.

The poems are curated by little angels of 6 to 16 years. The way they have sequenced their thoughts leaves an indelible mark on the readers, about their skillful writing. I especially like the way, they have expressed themselves in a raw, innocent yet gritty way. Though each poem gives wings to their imagination but Darshil, Devishi, Aadya, Aksha, Syeda and Shatakshi stand apart for their out-of-the-box thinking. The boutique of their poems is a treat to the soul.

Kshitij deserves praise for bringing these wonder kids together, so also their teachers and parents for nurturing them.

I would recommend the book for every student and adult to watch these budding poets fly to touch greater heights and get inspired.

Sh. Mukesh Bhatnagar
Author, Writer, Editor & Social Worker

Dishita Mahesh Joshi

Dishita Mahesh Joshi is a student of Sri Global School, Lucknow. Her mother is her inspiration and her father is her backbone. Her inclination is toward writing poems. She believes in speaking truth and is a straight-forward person.

Courage

Courage is not instantaneous,
Courage is miscellaneous.
Courage is overcoming fear,
Courage comes from a single tear.
Courage is self-belief,
Courage comes from grief.

When you face pain,
Then that's your own gain.
Next when you shout,
Your fear is ejected out.
Now whenever you fall,
Just dial a courageous call.

Aradhya Pandey

Aradhya Pandey is a teenager who loves to spend her time painting and writing.

She is creative, empathetic, curious and competitive. She likes to read a lot of books. She believes that the more you read, the more you know. Poetry is freedom for her, where people can actually find her heart. She dreams of having her own library for herself with all the books she cherishes more than any of her possessions. One of her favourite book quotes is "Love is a great beautifier" and she strongly agrees that affection and gentleness can work like magic to change someone's life forever.

Metamorphosis - True Beauty

Just like a curious little butterfly,

With your brittle yet fearless wings,

You reach up high in the sky.

You focus on the odds too often,

Keeping every infinity of possibilities caged inside.

Though you see no beauty,

Yet even your scars are shining,

As if striking lightning carved into the immense dark sky.

Oh, dear butterfly!

Live your life as you've desired,

Because you will always be truly admired.

Time goes by unapologetically.

Therefore, don't let your passionate dreams perish.

As the present too,

Will eventually become a memory to cherish.

Thus, fly higher each moment,

Take it all as if the world is yours to seize.

Hold your wings steady,

Be courageous, daring and inquisitive, enough to fly against even the strongest breeze.

Kajal Singh

Kajal Singh is a high school senior pursuing a PCB stream. She is an individual with a distinct and keen interest in literature, she enjoys writing poetry and reading. She uses literature as a tool to express her views on the world. Her other qualities include management and leadership, as a result, she has managed many events in her school life.

याद हो तुम सब

याद हो तुम सब और बातें भी तुम्हारी,

साथ है वह मीठी यादें भी हमारी,

कम नहीं था वह वक्त जो बिताया साथ था,

महीनों नहीं सालों तक एक दूसरे का साथ निभाया था,

वही कक्षा, वही बच्चे और चार हम,

कच्ची सी उम्र और पक्की से मित्रता हमारी,

याद हो तुम सब और बातें भी तुम्हारी।

वह झगड़ा वह रोना मेरा तुम्हारा,

सच, बहुत याद आती है तुम्हारी,

कट रही है जिंदगी कुछ नए दोस्तों के साथ,

पर वह बात नहीं जो थी तुम सबके साथ,

साल बीत गए तुम सब को देखे हुए,

पर यार, याद बहुत आती है तुम्हारी,

आकर याद बहुत सताती है तुम्हारी,

याद हो तुम सब और बातें भी तुम्हारी ।

Vishrant

Vishrant is a voracious reader. At the age of 10, he rediscovered his talent - the art of writing. The present poem, he has credited to his mother, for, it only happened when she asked him to write a poem. Today, the versatile Vishrant has developed a passion to read and write.

You

You are the first teacher of mine,

Who gave birth to this faded star and taught him
how to shine.

You, who made him the limit and kept no limit for
him.

You, who never did let his light be dim.

You, because of whom the first steps he took.

You, because of whom he travelled through the
galaxies which he had only seen in a book.

You, who taught him every word to speak,

Because of your pious scolds and slaps, his dreams
did not fade away.

You, who took to his mouth the chapatis and the
rice.

You, who tried your level best to make him nice.

You, who to make him sleep narrated those bed-
time stories.

You, the reason behind his glory.

Hats off to you, oh! selfless,

You, a mother, whom a dull star did bless.

Bhavya

A student of class 9, Bhavya dons various hats from being a chess player to a footballer to a photographer and a budding creative writer. He loves writing about nature and the environment.

आओ बचाएँ अपनी धरती

सूरज सोने-सा चमकीला,

आसमान मनमोहक नीला,

पंछियों का मीठा चहचहाना,

ठंडी हवाओं का कानों में गुनगुनाना ।

जब प्रकृति माँ कर रही अनेक जतन,

ताकि खुशहाल रहे हमारा जीवन

तो हम क्यों निरंतर कर रहे इसका पतन?

कहीं कट रहे वृक्ष, तो कहीं हो रह अवैध खनन!

आओ, सब मिलकर करें उपाय,

जिनसे धरती माँ को बचाया जाए,

चलो ले लें मिल कर सब प्रण,

कम करेंगे प्रदूषण ।

काटेंगे नहीं पेड़,

लगाएँगे नहीं प्लास्टिक का ढेर,

न करेंगे दूषित जल,

मिलकर बनाएँगे एक बेहतर कल।

जीवन जियेंगे इस प्रकार,

कि धरा को न लगे ज़रा भी भार,

खिलती रहे मेरी धरा,

और मनोरम बन जाए संसार ।

Syeda Amira Ali

Syeda Amira Ali is 6 years old and lives in Delhi. She is a grade 2 student of Bluebells School International. Her hobbies are reciting poems, singing, playing chess and talking with her friends.

मैं bluebells हूँ

मैम सोनी का बोया हुआ बीज

मैं bluebells हूँ

नित नई अपनी शाखाओं को फैलाता हुआ

मैम सुमन की बगिया का

मैं bluebells हूँ

सूरज की तरह रौशन अपना उजाला फैलाता हुआ

मैम किरन और मैम प्रन्या की आशाओं का समुंदर

मैं bluebells हूँ

अनंत तक अपने सपनों की उड़ान लिए हुए

मैम मंजु का

मैं bluebells हूँ

पायल मैम और आशिमा मैम की रुनझुन से मुस्कुराता हुआ

मैं bluebells हूँ

हरदम खुद को आगे बढ़ाने की धुन में मग्न

तन्मय सर का

मैं bluebells हूँ

जीत का जज़्बा हर दिन अपने दिल में लिए हुए

अजीत सर का

मैं bluebells हूँ

मीठी मीठी गुड़बानी लिए हुए मैम रिहाना और लूशीयस सर का

मैं bluebells हूँ।

पर्वत की शिखाओं सा अटल अपने बच्चों के भविष्य बनाने का इरादा रखने वाला मैम शिखा और मैम मनमीत का

मैं bluebells हूँ।

मेरी कोई सीमा नहीं मैं निरंतर प्रयासरत हूँ खुद को बेहतर बनाने में मैम सीमा का

मैं bluebells हूँ।

दीदी और गार्ड भैया के हौसले का

मैं bluebells हूँ।

सबके दिलों में राज करने वाला, रात के सपनों में आने वाला, सुबह की नींद उड़ाने वाला, दोस्तों से गपशप करवाने वाला, प्यारी प्यारी teachers से मिलवाने वाला मैं हम सबका प्यारा

bluebells हूँ।।

Shubhra Shukla

Shubhra Shukla is 6 years old and lives in Lucknow. She enjoys watching cartoons, playing with her younger brother and listening to stories by her grand-mother. She won a drawing competition in Russia in 2022. Her favorite color is pink and she likes to eat momos.

घर

घर में एक चिड़िया आयी,

पानी पीने रोज़ आयी,

मझ से खाना मांगती है,

की मै खुद अकेले खा लूँ

रोज़ रोज़,

अपने घोंसले मे जाती,

अपने बच्चों को खाना खिलाती

अगर बच्चे प्यासे होए

पानी मांगती है,

और बच्चों को पिलाती है

और सबसे ज़्यादा अपने बच्चों से प्यार करती है

Shatakshi Rai

Shatakshi is 12 years old and is studying in Class 8th. Her hobbies include dancing and drawing sketches. She loves to write.

Society

Roses aren't always red
And violets aren't exactly blue,
The society that we live in
Never seems to speak the truth.
Smiles aren't always happy
And frowns aren't always upset,
People judge too quickly
And our feelings are what they forget.

Geet Negi

Geet Negi likes to read, play basketball and badminton.

She loves trekking and adventure sports. She is interested in art and craft and also likes to travel to new places.

All I See

It's a place I love,

A place where I admire the green.

A meadow is its name,

Truly a wonderful sight to be seen.

Here the grass is green,

Surrounded with trees.

Here I wish

To sing and dance with the breeze.

Not even the rain,

Will bring me pain.

As long as there is a light,

And a meadow in sight.

The cat is on the prowl,

The squirrel runs up the tree.

But the dog is in its way

And I think,

Oh! there is always something

To see.

Darshil

Darshil is a curious 10-year-old with a heart full of adventure. He is a budding poet and an aspiring scientist, always eager to uncover the mysteries of the world. With a mischievous smile and twinkling eyes, Darshil is a natural explorer.

With a heart of gold, his kindness shines bright, making him a true friend to all. With his infectious laughter and contagious enthusiasm, he brings joy to everyone he meets.

कृतज्ञता

कृतज्ञता को आधार बनाना चाहता हूं

आभार व्यक्त करना चाहता हूं जीवन में।

बचपन से ही सीखना चाहता हूं

आभार व्यक्त करना चाहता हूं जीवन में।

दुनिया में मेरा अस्तित्व बनाने के लिए

परमात्मा का आभार व्यक्त करना चाहता हूं जीवन में।

जीवनदान और स्वास्थ्य दिया जिसने

प्रकृति का आभार व्यक्त करना चाहता हूं जीवन में।

जिंदगी और वास्ताविक प्रेम देनेवाले

माता पिता का आभार व्यक्त करना चाहता हूं जीवन में।

अक्षरज्ञान और सद्बुद्धि का दान देनेवाले

गुरु का आभार व्यक्त करना चाहता हूं जीवन में।

जीवन में सकारात्मक प्रभाव रखनेवाले

हर सजीव निर्जीव का आभार व्यक्त करना चाहता हूं जीवन में।

जो आज महसूस कर रहा हूं कृतज्ञता

उसे ही आज व्यक्त करना चाहता हूं जीवन में।

Medhanssh Srivastava

Medhanssh Srivastava loves poetry and playing piano. He was inspired by his principal to write poems. He is a keen observer and loves to play cricket.

Life is All About Certificates

Life is all about certificates......We get certificates
when we are born;

In this paper life goes on,

We get certificates for vaccination;

We get certificates on a destination,

Our school journey starts with certificates;

From character to migration;

competition to participation,

we get certificates.

On reaching college;

From one semester to another,

Again, we need certificates.

Now we need to do a job,

be ready with training and experience certificates;

it's the time to retire;

stand in a queue for pension

to get a life certificate,

Certificate ! Certificate ! Certificate!

Even Death also needs a Certificate!

Agampreet Singh

Agampreet Singh is an innocent child who is every teacher's delight. He expresses well in words. He loves discipline and has a knack for poetry writing.

My Kind Mother

Sometimes I think

Of my mother as a honeybee.

Doing her work regularly.

No time even to sleep.

Whenever I hug her

I feel that she is always with us.

She is always done with her chores,

And her company never bores.

Every morning she wakes up,

To cook food, to nurture.

Saving every penny for hers.

She truly cares for my future.

An embodiment of love, Ma!

Your heart is filled with compassion,

She is serious about her work.

It gives her the utmost satisfaction.

Always very caring,

motivating me for all the things.

I love you Mom from the bottom of my heart

For being so caring all along.

Atoofa Parveen

Atoofa Parveen is a student of Shri Ram Global School. She has a keen interest in writing poems based on real-life situations and get inspiration from them. She has often won many awards in this field. Besides this, she is a good artist and calligrapher as well!

Manoj Kumar Pandey

"If Death Strikes before I prove my

Blood, I swear I'll kill death."

Yes, I am the real hero!

I proved my blood,

I was killed in Kargil War.

Yes, I am the real hero!

I embraced death which tasted sweeter than honey,

I sacrificed my life so millions of Indians could live
in peace.

Yes, I am the real hero!

I was a true Indian,

I was an army officer,

Yes, I am the real hero!

I wanted to win Param Vir Chakra,

I had Eleven Gorkha Rifles,

Yes, I am Captain Manoj Kumar Pandey!

Yes, I am the real hero!

Daniel

Daniel is studying in class 11 and is pursuing science. He is passionate about serving his nation. He loves reading books, and his favourite genres are Greek mythology and world history.

The Aviator

The light outside starts fading, retreating.

The sky turns orange, it looks divine.

His heart is beating, he has a nervous feeling.

All as he is looking at the sky.

He suits up, has a light snack to eat.

As he is looking up high,

The eyes of confidence he finally meets,

All as he is looking at the sky.

He says a quick prayer,

He feels his troubles, far away fly.

He loses all his fears,

All as he is looking at the sky.

As he is walking towards the hangar,

He feels his spirits rise.

His mind becomes clear,

All as he is looking at the sky.

He sits in his seat, starts the engine,

Showing in their spinning, all their might.

He talks to the controllers, he carefully listens,

He will soon be in the sky.

On the suit that he wears,

It is written on his shoulders' stripes,

That he has conquered all his fears,

They lead him to the sky.

With only God as his protector,

He has flown through the most treacherous of nights,

And Has emerged as a Victor,

All while he was in the sky.

As he gets ready again, today,

He is ready as always to die.

He increases speed, the wind gives way,

He is now in the sky.

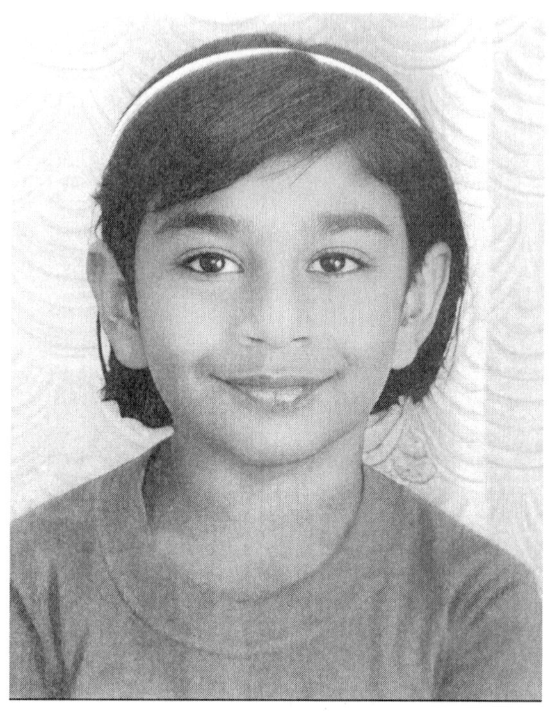

Aksha Asthana

Aksha Asthana is 8 years old studying in grade 3 in DPS Neelbad, Bhopal. She has received the Shining Star student award in all her previous classes. She has a keen interest in creative writing.

My Favourite Colours - the Colours of Nature

My favourite colours are the colours of nature. They give me joy and are very special.

When the sun rises, its beautiful hues make me happy as can be.

The green of the trees, fluttering with the breeze,

they help us breathe, clean fresh air.

The blue of the sky and the ocean too. The white of the clouds floating by,

when the clouds pour, they quench our thirst.

The yellow of the sunflower and the pink rose,

make me smile with all their beauty.

When it is night, the glittering stars,

shine and glow.

The silver moon has all the glory,

which makes me so happy.

It is our duty to protect this nature,

and give it our best, for a great future.

Devishi Mathur

Devishi Mathur, a 17 year old budding writer, is studying in Dubai. She has been writing poems since the age of 10.

She has a stable interest in crafts and extra-curriculars, making her a student with various abilities.

She tries to be the best of who she can and works towards achieving her best potential.

Altruism

Spread a little benevolence,

Everywhere you go.

Let that little goodness,

From your heart, flow.

Kind souls are the mesmerizing gardens,

Kind thoughts are the hidden roots.

Kind words are the surface blooms,

Kind deeds are the luscious fruits.

Love in the sweet sunshine,

That swelters into life.

For only in obscurity, we whine,

Grows animosity and strife.

Oh, things like these,

These little things,

Puts us at soothed ease,

And to our souls, adds wings.

The transparent love discloses,

As aromatic atoms in the air,

Reveal the latent rose,

Altruism is here, altruism is there.

Toshani Ojha

Toshani Ojha is a cheerful 8 year old girl studying in grade 4, Timpany School, Visakhapatnam. She loves painting, reading story-books by Sudha Murthy and trying her hands in various craft forms.

नेताजी सुभाष चंद्र बोस

आज सुनाती हूँ गाथा

एक वीर जवान की

देश के आज़ादी के लिए

जिसके खून मे

बेमिसाल उबाल था।

निर्भीक निडर

पूजे जाते है आज भी घर घर

'तुम मुझे खून दो, मे तुम्हे दूंगा आज़ादी'

जिनका था क्रांतिकारी नारा।

भारत माँ के बेटे सुभाष

हम सबका प्यारा

जिस देश का ऐसा बेटा हो

कैसे रह सकता वह मिटटी गुलाम ?

आज़ादी के लिए हँसते हँसते

खुद हुए कुर्बान

नेताजी आपके देशप्रेम के आगे

शीश झुका के करते नमन

आज भी हम जवान।

Aarna

Aarna is 9 year old and is very creative. She likes to create her own cartoon characters and sing rap songs. She likes to learn musical instruments such as Drums.

She is a student of 5th standard at Suchitra Academy, Secunderabad.

Clouds

Clouds, Clouds, you give us rain.

You are many shapes in the sky.

You stay on top of the high.

You are sometimes black,

And sometimes white,

Sometimes small,

And sometimes big.

You are everywhere.

When air blows,

They play with the flow.

Clouds, Clouds, you give us rain.

Clouds, you are powerful.

They stop the sunlight.

Sometimes, they shine with sunlight.

You look like cotton candy,

I can touch you from high mountains.

Aadya

Aadya is a child prodigy who excels in multiple art forms - singing, music, sketching, writing and public speaking. She has won many accolades for her performances in music, dance, debates, poetry and video making. She has been featured in a leading daily Dainik Bhaskar for her achievements and a high point for her came when the IMF Chief Economist Ms. Gita Gopinath appreciated her on Twitter for decoding negative oil prices theory. She studies in 8th standard in Vasudev C Wadhwa Arya Vidya Mandir School, Mumbai.

Decades To Now

Decades ago, the earth blossomed.

Decades after, it struggles with hundred different
problems.

Decades ago, people were cautious.

Decades after, the people are obnoxious.

What have we done?! Look for yourself.

And then answer… was it selfish or selfless?

Compare the behaviour, the wrongs and rights,

Think beyond your thoughts, see beyond your sight,

And just maybe we can make it right.

Global warming, they say, is nothing about it to
worry.

Well, if you won't act on it fast, to another planet
you must scurry.

Reduce, Recycle, Reuse.

They are more than words; they are actions we do.

So, listen to us who actually say,

Hurting nature is a heavy price to pay.

Heed this warning, and take appropriate actions,

Actions that help and bring satisfaction.

Neerja Mahesh Bhatia

Neerja Mahesh Bhatia is 11 years old. She is studying in Rachana School, Ahmedabad, Gujarat.

आज़ाद परिंदे

हम हैं आज़ाद परिंदे,

माना माँ का आँचल,

पिता का साथ, गुरु का ज्ञान है।

यहीं तो हौसला बुलंद है।

मंजिल ऊन्ही को मिलती है,

जिसके ख्यालो में जोश है।

पंख नहीं सिर्फ उड़ान के लिए,

धैर्य और निर्णय भी जरूरी है।

ना डराओ हमें की लड़की है तू,

पंछी भी पंख आते ही उड़ जाते हैं।

कुछ कर दिखाना है

सिर्फ नौ इंच के मोबाइल पर नहीं सब के दिलो पर छा जाना है।

बेलन, चरखा न दिखाओ डरा कर

हम बोझ नहीं सबके, सिर का ताज है।

मैं तो वह नीरजा हूं, जो पानी में भी संवर जाती हूं।

बस हौसले मेरे बुलंद है,

क्षितिज का सरताज बनना चाहती हूं।

हम हैं आज़ाद परिंदे !

Aayesha John

Aayesha John is a student of class 6. She has a passion for writing, singing, dancing, painting, badminton and dramatics. She has participated and won awards in several of these artistic endeavours.

Matter Around Us

Oh, matter, matter!

So much to tell about you.

You have different states,

Sometimes solid, sometimes liquid and gas.

Solid like a stick.

Sometimes, it falls like a brick.

Liquid-like water which can get spilled.

Gases like air and oxygen do have mass.

Some things that really matter are

ice changing to water;

water changing to vapour;

and water changing into ice again

Oh, matter, matter!

All around us.

You are everywhere

from tea-cup to bag.

Some have lustre while others have texture.